SCORING IN RUGBY

To win a game you need to score more points than the opposing team, and you need to be able help your team to score those points. You can only score points in the following four ways:

1 Touching the ball down behind the opposition try line = 5 points (called a try).
2 Kicking the ball (which is placed on the ground) between the posts and over the cross bar after a try has been scored (called a conversion) = 2 points. The kick has to be taken in line with where the try was scored.
3 Kicking the ball through the posts but above the cross bar with the ball placed on the ground when your team has been awarded a penalty = 3 points.
4 Kicking the rugby ball between the posts on the half volley (called a drop goal) = 3 points.

The posts in rugby look like the letter "H" with two upright posts and a cross bar between them.

Rugby is a highly exciting game, full of energy and pace.

Do you want to play professional rugby, earning fame and fortune? Perhaps you can imagine playing rugby for your country in front of thousands of people, or maybe you just want to play the game well and enjoy it.

Whatever your ambitions, you need to start by learning some very important basic skills (called key skills) and, if you become really good at them, it will allow you to play the best rugby you can.

This book is designed to help you progress by providing a series of key skills. These include passing, catching and kicking practices that you can do in your back garden or a nearby open space, either on your own, with a friend, or with your brother, sister, mum or dad!

All you need is a rugby ball (size 3 or 4 are the best sizes until you are a teenager) and something to mark out a small area – it could be your hat, scarf or jumper if you have nothing else.

You need to practise each skill regularly, even after you become good at it! This book will show you ways to challenge yourself by making practices harder.

Please remember that, because the rugby ball is shaped like an egg, when it bounces it can go in any direction. This is part of the fun, but you should be careful to practise where the ball won't cause any damage or go into a road if it bounces in an unexpected direction.

WHAT MAKES A GOOD RUGBY PLAYER?

- Concentration
- Confidence
- Fitness
- Quick reactions and foot movement
- Good handling of the ball
- Ability to 'read' the game and adapt accordingly
- Courage

In a maul, one of the players will have hold of the ball.

FORWARD PASS
When a player passes the ball forwards to a teammate.

LINE OUT
The line out is a way of restarting the game after the ball has gone into touch (off the field of play at the side). Like the scrum, the line out gets all the forwards in one place near to the touch line, so the backs have space to run in.

BACKS
These are the players who receive the ball from the forwards and they try to run and score.

THREE QUARTERS
Another name for the Backs.

RUCK
A ruck is when a group of players are trying to push each other off a ball on the ground in order to gain possession.

MAUL
This is the same as a ruck only this time one of the group will be holding the ball.

TOUCH LINE
The line which runs up the side of the pitch.

TRY LINE
The line which runs across the end of the pitch.

BE THE BEST
Learning these terms by heart will help to improve your skills, as you will be able to concentrate fully on your coach's instructions instead of struggling to work out what he is talking about!

POSITIONS IN **RUGBY**

There are 15 players in the usual rugby team, although there are fewer players in some versions of rugby. Seven-a-side is an exciting game, with its own World Cup, and there is also a 10-a-side game. Young players have fewer members on each team so that there is more chance to run with the ball. Here we will look at the positions in 15-a-side rugby.

A rugby team is split into forwards and backs. The Forwards contest for the ball with the opposition team's Forwards and then give it to their Backs, who try to get past the opposition players to score. Backs tend to be a little lighter than Forwards so that, if they win the ball, they can run fast.

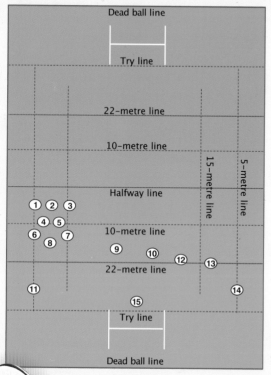

FORWARDS

No.	Name
1	Loosehead Prop
2	Hooker
3	Tighthead Prop
4	Lock or Second Row
5	Lock or Second Row
6	Blindside Flanker
7	Openside Flanker
8	Number Eight

BACKS

No.	Name
9	Scrum Half
10	Fly Half
11	Wing
12	Inside Centre
13	Outside Centre
14	Wing
15	Fullback

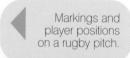

Markings and player positions on a rugby pitch.

Let's look at what each position requires:

1 LOOSEHEAD PROP

- Is strong in the scrum and so helps the Hooker.
- Is a strong support player at the line out.
- Is a strong tackler – tackles the man and the ball.
- Has the ability to stay on his feet and pass in contact.
- Pushes hard at the rucks and mauls.

2 HOOKER

- Can throw in to the lineout accurately.
- Wins the ball in the scrum.
- Runs around the pitch quickly.
- Is a strong runner with the ball.
- Is the boss of the scrum.

3 TIGHTHEAD PROP

- Is the strong man (the rock) of the scrum.
- Is a strong runner with the ball over short distances.
- Normally a 'square-shaped' player – big shoulders and strong legs.
- Has the ability to stay on his feet and pass in contact.
- Is a strong tackler – tackles the man and the ball.

4 & 5 LOCKS (SECOND ROW)

- Has the ability to jump in line out.
- Is fast around the pitch.
- Is a strong physical presence.
- Is an aggressive defender.

You need to be a strong runner to be a Hooker, like England star Lee Mears.

6 BLINDSIDE FLANKER

- Line out option – can jump.
- Is a strong runner with the ball.
- Has a huge work-rate.
- Is a good defender.

7 OPENSIDE FLANKER

- Dominates tackle and collision areas.
- Links forwards and backs.
- Is an extremely fit, fast player.
- Is a skilful ball player who wins the ball in rucks and mauls.

8 NUMBER EIGHT

- Has a huge work-rate.
- Is a good defender.
- Is a strong communicator and decision-maker.
- Is a strong runner with the ball.
- Understands and plans team options.

9 SCRUM HALF

- Is a quick, long, accurate passer.
- Has a huge work rate.
- Is the 'general' of the forwards.
- Is an accurate kicker.
- Understands all the team moves.

10 FLY HALF

- Is an accurate and quick passer with both hands.
- Is a threat to opposition defensive lines.
- Has all-round good kicking skills.
- Is a good decision-maker under pressure.
- Is one of the team leaders.

11 & 14 WING

- Is a very fast runner.
- Is good at scoring tries.
- Is good at swerving/side-stepping.
- Can ead the other team's defence and defends accurately.
- Can catch a high ball under pressure.
- Can kick well under pressure.

12 & 13 CENTRE

- Is a sharp and evasive runner.
- Is fast over 20 metres.
- Is a good kicker.
- Is a good passer off both hands.

15 FULL BACK

- Has kicking skills with either foot.
- Can catch a high ball under pressure.
- Is a fast and strong runner.
- Can run into space in attack.
- Communicates defence and defends accurately.

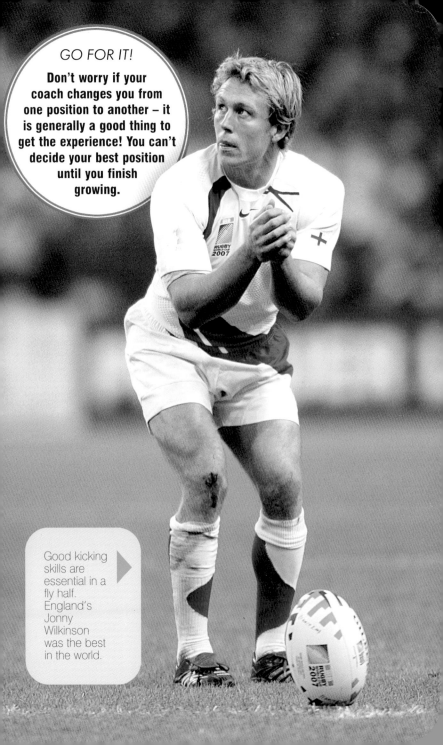

GO FOR IT!

Don't worry if your coach changes you from one position to another – it is generally a good thing to get the experience! You can't decide your best position until you finish growing.

Good kicking skills are essential in a fly half. England's Jonny Wilkinson was the best in the world.

PASSING

Whatever position you play, you will need to be able to pass the ball quickly and accurately. It is one of the basic skills of rugby – and it is not quite as simple as it looks. Top players practise all the time to perfect their passing and their ability to catch the ball, often when running at speed. Use these drills to help you become a reliable passer and catcher.

Passing practice

You will need:
- Two or three players.
- A rugby ball.
- A small area (10 paces by 10 paces).

Key points

- Run around the area in any direction passing the ball between each other.

- How many passes can you make in 30 seconds while staying at least 2 metres away from each other?
- Try to pass using your fingers behind the ball to flick it to your partner. This makes the ball go faster.
- Try different ways of passing: catch and pass the ball with your hands above your head, or catch and pass the ball with your hands below your knees.
- How many can you do without dropping the ball?

Make it harder

Instead of passing in any direction you now need to practise passing to the side and slightly behind you, as forward passes are not allowed in rugby.

Using the same small area try running alongside your partner across the area. The ball carrier

Lateral pass: The most common pass used in rugby.

should be slightly in front. When the pass is made, the player with the ball runs slightly faster so that they are in front of the player who just passed the ball. The player who just passed the ball should slow up a little to allow the new ball carrier to overtake him.

LATERAL (SIDEWAYS) PASS

This pass is the most common and is used when you pass the ball to a team mate running alongside and just behind you. Remember to slow slightly after you have passed the ball.

Key points
- Run straight, holding the ball in two hands.
- Look at the player who will receive the pass.
- Swing your arms towards him and follow through so that your fingers on both hands end up pointing towards the receiver.

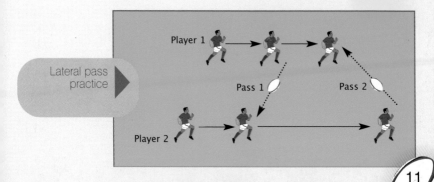

Lateral pass practice

Player 1

Pass 1

Pass 2

Player 2

- Pass the ball at chest height in front of the receiver.
- Support the new ball carrier (i.e. be within passing distance in case he needs to pass the ball).

RUNNING AND PASSING

- Run straight – if you run across the pitch you may not be going forwards!
- Hold the ball in both hands – if you hold it under one arm you cannot pass properly.
- Commit a defender – run towards the left side of the defender if you are passing to the right (see diagram opposite) so that the defender is drawn across, which creates space for your teammate to run into.
- Turn your upper body side-on to the defence, to face the supporting receiver.
- Swing your arms through in the direction of the pass.
- Use your elbows and wrists to control the speed and flight of the ball as it is released.
- Follow through with your hands in the direction of the pass.
- Pass to the 'target' area, which is at chest height in front of the receiver.
- Support the receiver once the pass has been completed by remaining in passing distance.

Running and passing: Swing your arms through in the direction of the pass.

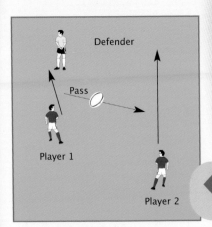

Defender

Pass

Player 1

Player 2

BE THE BEST

Rugby balls are notoriously easy to drop. Reduce the risk of this by reaching out to the ball in plenty of time and using your fingers like a funnel, 'feeding' the ball into the palms of your hands.

When you are running and passing, commit a defender by running to his left if you are passing to the right.

CATCHING A PASS

- Position yourself so that you can run towards the ball in its flight.
- Run towards the space created by the passer drawing the defender towards him.
- Call for the ball.
- Reach with your hands to catch the ball early.
- Watch the ball into your hands.
- Catch the ball with your fingers and hands.
- Get ready to pass to another member of your team.

SPIN PASS

If you make the ball spin when you pass it, it will travel further and faster through the air. But it can also make the ball harder to catch, so only use a spin pass when you want to pass over a longer distance than normal. The best example of this is the scrum half pass (see page 16).

Key points

- Hold the ball in both hands with the point facing up.
- Put your hands on either side of the ball so that you are holding it at its widest part.
- Throw the ball about half a metre into the air and catch it again.
- Use your strong hand (right if you are right handed) to 'roll' the ball as it leaves your hands.
- Repeat this until you can throw the ball high so that it spins in the air and lands in your hands without tumbling – the ball should spin around but should stay with the point-up.

13

Now, stand facing a partner and pass to each other so the ball spins as it did when you were throwing it to yourself.

Key points
- Position yourself exactly as you would for a lateral pass.
- Hold the ball so the point is facing towards the receiver.
- Look at the player who will receive the pass.
- Swing your arms towards him and let the ball roll out of your right hand (if you are passing to the left) or left hand (if you are passing to the right).
- Follow through with the fingers of both your hands, so that they finish up pointing towards the receiver.
- Pass the ball at chest height in front of the receiver.

Make it harder
- Start a metre or so away. Every time you both catch the ball move one step backwards.
- If one of you drops the ball take one step towards each other.
- See how far you can pass it without dropping the ball.
- Then run across a small area passing sideways to each other, as you did with the lateral pass, but gradually move further away from each other.

OVERHEAD PASS
Sometimes in a game you may need to pass the ball over the head(s) of players to one of your teammates who is in space and has no one in front of him. This is called an overhead pass.

You will need:
- Three players.
- A rugby ball.
- A small area (10 paces by 10 paces).

Practice
- Run around the area in any direction, passing the ball between two of you with the third player trying to catch the ball (piggy in the middle).

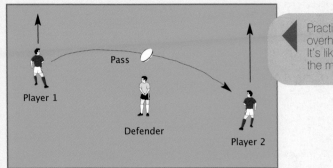

Pass

Player 1

Defender

Player 2

Practising the overhead pass: It's like piggy in the middle.

- The receiver needs to keep moving so that the player in the middle can't get between you.
- If the player in the middle catches the ball or it is dropped, swap the player in the middle.

- Try to make the pass using your fingers to spin the ball to your partner.
- Now try to pass over the head of the player in the middle, but remember that the receiver still has to move around.

Overhead pass.

SCRUM HALF PASS

This is called a scrum half pass because the scrum half uses this pass the most as the link between the forwards and the backs.

During a game of rugby, however, there are often occasions when a group of players are all in one part of the field together, normally in a ruck or a maul. The player arriving last to the group will need to pass the ball, maybe from the ground, away quickly and over some distance to a teammate. Therefore, every player on the team needs to be able to pass the ball this way, from a position that is low to the ground.

Practice 1

You will need:
- Two of you – if you are on your own you can use a wall to pass against.
- A rugby ball.

Key points
- Put the ball on the ground so that the point is facing in the direction you are passing.

Scrum half pass: Crouch low to pick up the ball from the ground. Remember to follow through with both arms so that they end up pointing towards the receiver.

- Put your rear foot beside the ball – it should be your right foot if you are passing to your left.
- Make sure your feet are wide apart so that you can get down to the ball.
- Put both your hands on the wide part of the ball with the point pointing in the direction you want to pass.
- Sweep the ball towards your target (the hands of the receiver or a point on a wall if you are on your own).
- Let the ball roll off the fingers of your right hand (if passing to the left) or left hand (if passing to the right).
- Follow through with the fingers of both your hands so that they end up pointing towards the receiver.
- Pass the ball at chest height in front of the receiver.

Make it harder

- Try to sweep the ball away from you as soon as you touch it (without picking it up and moving it backwards before you pass).
- Increase the distance you are passing.
- Get the receiver to run on to your pass. You will need to pass in front of him.

Practice 2

If there are three of you, you will need:
- A rugby ball
- Four cones or markers (you can use anything that isn't sharp).

Key points

- Mark out a square with a marker on each corner.
- Each of you stands on a different corner, leaving one free.
- One of you has the ball at your feet.
- Make a scrum half pass to the nearest player, then run in the opposite direction to the spare corner (see photos opposite).
- The next player does the same thing – passing one way and then running the other.

As soon as you pass the ball, run to the next cone.

Make it harder

- Try to pass around the square four times without dropping the ball.
- Time yourselves – how many passes can you make in 30 seconds or one minute, for example?
- Increase the distance you are passing by making the square bigger.

French scrum half Morgan Parra gathers the ball from a scrum and executes a perfect scrum half pass. Notice his grip on the ball.

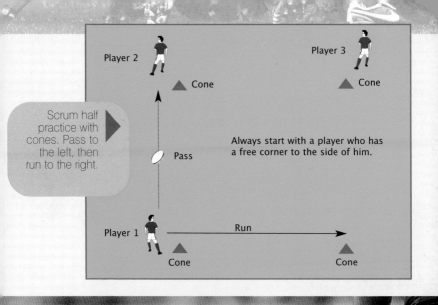

Player 2

▲ Cone

Player 3

▲ Cone

Scrum half practice with cones. Pass to the left, then run to the right.

Pass

Always start with a player who has a free corner to the side of him.

Player 1

Run

▲ Cone

▲ Cone

CATCHING

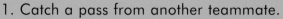

R ugby is a handling game, which means that you will need to be good at catching the ball. You may need to:

1. Catch a pass from another teammate.
2. Intercept a pass made by the opposition.
3. Catch a kick made by either a teammate or the opposing team.

CATCHING A HIGH BALL

You will need:
• Just you to start with.
• A rugby ball.

Key points

• Without a ball, point your hands up to the sky, stretching them above your head. If you move your bottom hand out a little way from your body this will give you the best position for catching a high ball.
• Now hold a rugby ball in both hands and make sure you have plenty of space around you.
• Throw the ball up above your head and catch it as it comes down by reaching both your hands up towards the ball, remembering the first position.

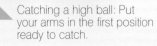

Catching a high ball: Put your arms in the first position ready to catch.

- See if you can catch the ball by pulling it down rather than letting it hit your hands.
- See if you can catch the ball softly, without it making a sound.

GO FOR IT!

Throw the ball a little higher each time you practise, making sure you catch the ball softly. See how high you can go.

2

3

 Pull the ball in rather than letting it hit your hands.

 Receive the ball into your body, ready to pass to another player.

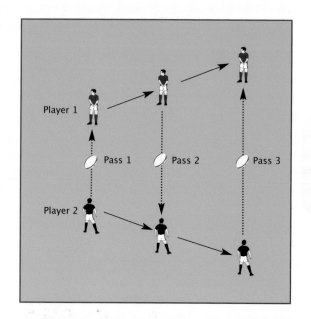

Player 1

Pass 1   Pass 2   Pass 3

Player 2

Catching practice with a partner. See if you can move further apart.

Make it harder

- Ask a partner to join you and take turns throwing the ball up to each other.
- Gradually move further apart, but be careful to make sure you have plenty of space around you both.
- Once you are catching the ball confidently, try a little competition. Each time you catch the ball move one step further apart. How far can you get before dropping the ball?
- Try this same competition, but punt kick the ball to each other instead (see page 29).

CATCHING A PASS IN THREES

You will need:
- A rugby ball.
- Two partners to practise with you.

Key points

- Stand in a line two metres away from each other, all facing in the same direction.
- Pass the ball to the middle player.
- The receiver reaches out so that he takes the ball early, spreading his fingers wide.

- Keep your eyes open and watch the ball until it is safely in his hands.
- The pass should be made at chest height.
- Now pass back and forth between the three of you, making sure that you all reach with both hands to pull the ball in rather than allowing it to hit your hands.
- When making a pass, swing your arms across your body and release the ball towards the receiver.
- If you are the player in the middle, can you catch the ball and pass it on in one swinging movement?

Make it harder

- Move a little further away.
- Once you are catching the ball confidently, try a competition. Each time you catch the ball move a step further apart. How far can you get without dropping the ball?
- Now try jogging together in line and passing the ball as you go.
- Gradually speed up, but be sure to pass backwards. The way to do this is to slow a little when you have made the pass and to speed up a little when you have the ball.
- Take turns to be the middle player. It is the hardest position, but gives you the best practice!

Catching a pass in threes.

KICKING

Although rugby is mainly a running and passing game, there are times when you need to kick. There are five main types of kick:

1 A drop kick: To start the game or to score three points.

2 A place kick: To score a conversion after a try has been scored (see page 3) or to kick a penalty.

3 Chip kick: To beat a defender by kicking over or around him.

4 A punt kick: A kick into space or to relieve pressure by finding touch (kicking the ball over the touch line).

5 A grubber kick: Kicking the ball along the ground to beat defenders or find space.

When practising your kicking you should remember to check the following:

- Make sure you have a strong pair of rugby boots on. Kicking with soft footwear may hurt your feet!

- The rugby ball bounces in odd directions because of its shape, so make sure you have plenty of space around you.
- Warm up before you start practising so that you don't injure yourself.

DID YOU KNOW?

The first ever international rugby match took place on March 27, 1871, in Edinburgh between Scotland and England. The hosts won.

DROP KICK

You will need:
- A rugby ball.
- Space to practise in.

Key points

- Hold the ball so that it points downwards with your hands on either side of it.

- Keep your head and shoulders still, and hold the ball over your foot so that the point of the ball is slightly towards you.
- Step forward and plant the foot that you are not kicking with firmly on the ground.
- Drop the ball on to its point on the ground.
- Kick the ball with the top of your foot just after it has hit the ground – too early and the ball will bump along the ground (see grubber kick on page 31) – too late and you will miss it.
- Swing your leg through the ball so it pops up into the air.

- Try to keep your balance by holding out the opposite arm to your kicking foot (right footed = left arm out for balance).
- Keep swinging your foot up after you have kicked the ball, and keep your head down until the ball is in the air.
- To start with, just practise kicking the ball a little way in the air.

Make it harder
- Have a bench or similar low target to kick over.

Drop kick: 1. Hold the ball above your foot.
2. Drop the ball and kick it just after it hits the ground, following through with your leg.

- Try to get the ball higher each time.
- Pick a higher target (such as a washing line, but check with your parents or guardians first), and try standing close to it, but still drop kick the ball over the target.

PLACE KICK

You will need:
- A rugby ball.
- A lot of space to practise in.

Key points
- Place the ball on the ground on a slightly raised mound of mud (you can use the heel of your boot to create this).
- Lean the ball slightly forwards, as this will give you the wide part of the ball (the sweet spot) to hit.
- Keeping your head and shoulders still, stand over the ball with your kicking foot behind the ball.
- Walk backwards a few paces. Keep your eye on the sweet spot of the ball.
- Take a few deep breaths and focus on the sweet spot.
- Walk forward to the ball and plant the foot that you are not kicking with firmly on the ground next to the ball.
- Turn the shoulder opposite to your kicking foot towards the target.

Place kick: Swing your kicking leg through the ball as you strike it, holding out your opposite arm to keep your balance.

26

GO FOR IT!

Improve the accuracy of your place kick by aiming for a target. How many times in a row can you kick the ball into your target area?

- Swing your kicking foot through the ball, keeping your head down.
- Sweep the ball away by hitting it with the inside of your foot.
- Keep your balance by holding out the arm opposite to your kicking foot.
- Keep swinging your foot up, even after you have kicked the ball, and keep your head down until the ball is in the air.
- To start with, just practise kicking the ball a little way with a two- or three-pace run up.

As you improve your place kick, try increasing the distance you aim for.

CHIP KICK

This is used to kick the ball over a defender's head. You should start by practising from a standing position.

Key points

- Keep your eyes on the ball.
- With your head and shoulders still, hold the ball over your foot so that the point of the ball is slightly towards you.
- Step forward and plant the foot that you are not kicking with firmly on the ground.
- Drop the ball on to your kicking foot with your dominant hand (your right hand if you are right-handed).
- Swing your leg through the ball so it pops up into the air.
- Try to keep your balance so that you don't fall over.
- Keep your foot pointing straight ahead, and don't tilt it up towards your head.

Chip kick:
1. Drop the ball on to your kicking foot and swing your leg through to meet it.
2. The ball should 'chip' through the air over the head of the defending player.
3. Keeping your eyes on the ball, run around the defender to gather it.

- Keep swinging your foot up even after you have kicked the ball, and keep your head down until the ball is in the air.
- To start with, just practise kicking the ball a little way in the air. See if you can catch it again without having to run too far ahead.

Make it harder

- See if you can walk along, kick the ball up and catch it again.
- Now try jogging – it will take quite a few goes to get this right.
- If you can, use a small bush or chair as a defender.
- Remember, start slowly and gradually build up your speed until you can run at the defender and pop the ball up with your foot and then run

around and catch it on the other side.
- If there are two of you, take turns being the defender. At first, the defender should not try to intercept the ball, but as the kicker gets more proficient the defender can try to stop it by raising his hands. Then the attacker needs to kick a little higher!

PUNT KICK

This is similar to the chip kick, but you will be trying to get much more height and distance on the ball. Try to kick the ball towards a target, such as a jumper on the ground, but it should be no more than a few metres away to start with. Make sure there is plenty of room to practise your kicking and that there are no windows near by!

Key points

- Put your hands on either side of the ball.
- Point the toe of your kicking foot.
- If you are kicking with your right foot, put your left shoulder forward.
- Place your non-kicking foot firmly on the ground, lined up towards your target.
- Drop the ball on to your foot as it swings through.
- Kick the ball towards the target before it drops too far.
- Hit the ball along its length and not at the point.
- Swing your kicking foot through after kicking the ball towards the target.
- Hold out the arm opposite your kicking foot to help you to keep your balance.

Make it harder

- See if you can make the ball travel higher by kicking it later as your foot swings through.
- Kick over a bench or a similar obstacle and see if you can still land the ball on the target.
- Move further away from the target, but make sure you keep landing the ball near it every time.
- If you can get a partner to join you, take turns kicking to each other and see how far you can move back before your kicking becomes inaccurate. This is a good way for you to practise your catching skills as well as improving your kicking.

Punt kick: 1. Pointing your toes, drop the ball on to your kicking foot.
2. Follow through your kick to improve the accuracy of your aim.

GRUBBER KICK

This is kicking the ball along the ground to beat a defender. Again, begin by practising this while you are standing still.

Key points

- Put your hands on either side of the ball.
- Point the toe of your kicking foot towards the ground.
- Make sure your weight is over the top of the ball.
- Drop the ball on to your foot as it swings through.
- Push the ball forwards on to the ground with a short, stabbing kick.
- Follow the kick through with your foot.
- The ball should bounce a metre or so in front of you before bouncing along the ground.

BE THE BEST

Once you are good at the grubber kick from a standing position, practise it at jogging speed then at running speed. This will give you the ability to perform the move during the pace of a real match.

Make it harder

- Use a small bush or chair as a defender.
- Remember; start slowly and gradually build up your speed until you can run at the defender and stab the ball past him with your foot, then run around and catch it as it bounces along.
- If there are two of you, take turns being the defender.

Grubber kick:
Kicking the ball along the ground to get around a defender.

THE LAST **WORD**

Practise all these key skills and gradually they will become second nature to you. You will not have to think about being able to do them in a game – you will see the opportunity and then perform the skill automatically.

The top players practise key skills every day...and so must you if you want to be like them.

First published 2009 by
A & C Black Publishers Ltd
36 Soho Square, London W1D 3QY
www.acblack.com

Copyright © 2009 Westline Publishing

ISBN: 978-1-4081-1410-0

Note: It is always the responsibility of the individual to assess his or her own fitness capability before participating in any training activity. Whilst every effort has been made to ensure the content of this book is as technically accurate as possible, neither the author nor the publishers can accept responsibility for any injury or loss sustained as a result of the use of this material.

A CIP catalogue record for this book is available from the British Library.

Text and cover design by Westline Publishing Ltd

Photography: PA Photos,(incl. Cover), istockphoto.com and Julia Barnes.

Special thanks to: Issy Johns-Turner, Rebecca Thompson, Yaz Dell,Toby Webb, Carl Manley, Tom Watts, Kane Frith, Charlie Gwyther, Ross Horman, and Ben Hobbs.

This book is produced using paper that is made from wood grown in managed, sustainable forests. It is natural, renewable and recyclable. The logging and manufacturing processes conform to the environmental regulations of the country of origin.

Typeset in the UK

Printed and bound in Singapore by Tien Wah Press.

KNOW THE GAME SKILLS

RUGBY

Tackling, Contact, Teamwork, Tactics

■ Key Techniques ■ Equipment ■ Advice for Learners ■ Rules of the Game

If you enjoyed this book, you should also read its companion volume, *Rugby: Tackling, Contact, Teamwork, Tactics*, available from all good book shops, priced £4.99.

A NOTE ON GENDER
Although the 'he' pronoun is used throughout this book, no gender bias is intended.